MW01013038

EUROPEAN STYLE
KITCHEN DESIGN

TINA SKINNER

EUROPEAN STYLE
KITCHEN DESIGNS

TINA SKINNER

Schiffer
Publishing Ltd

4880 Lower Valley Road Atglen, Pennsylvania 19310

Copyright © 2006 by Schiffer Publishing Ltd.
Library of Congress Control Number: 2006938392

All rights reserved. No part of this work may be re-
produced or used in any form or by any means—graphic,
electronic, or mechanical, including photocopying or
information storage and retrieval systems—without
written permission from the publisher.

The scanning, uploading and distribution of this
book or any part thereof via the Internet or via any other
means without the permission of the publisher is illegal
and punishable by law. Please purchase only authorized
editions and do not participate in or encourage the
electronic piracy of copyrighted materials.

"Schiffer," "Schiffer Publishing Ltd. & Design," and
the "Design of pen and ink well" are registered trade-
marks of Schiffer Publishing Ltd.

Front cover image *Courtesy of Wood Mode, Inc.*
Back cover image *Courtesy of Wood Mode, Inc.*

Designed by John P. Cheek
Cover design by Bruce Waters
Type set in Arrus BT/Adobe Jenson Pro

ISBN: 0-7643-2607-4
Printed in China

Published by Schiffer Publishing Ltd.
4880 Lower Valley Road
Atglen, PA 19310
Phone: (610) 593-1777; Fax: (610) 593-2002
E-mail: Info@schifferbooks.com

For the largest selection of fine reference books on
this and related subjects, please visit our web site at
www.schifferbooks.com
We are always looking for people to write books on
new and related subjects. If you have an idea for a
book please contact us at the above address.

This book may be purchased from the publisher.
Include $3.95 for shipping.
Please try your bookstore first.
You may write for a free catalog.

In Europe, Schiffer books are distributed by
Bushwood Books
6 Marksbury Ave.
Kew Gardens
Surrey TW9 4JF England
Phone: 44 (0) 20 8392-8585;
Fax: 44 (0) 20 8392-9876
E-mail: info@bushwoodbooks.co.uk
Website: www.bushwoodbooks.co.uk
Free postage in the U.K., Europe; air mail at cost.

Contents

Old World for The New

Today's homeowners have more choices facing them than ever before. The world is open to them in terms of imports, and the sky is the limit in terms of craftsmanship. In addition, pride in home is at an all-time high, and today's designers are raising the bar on quality and appearance.

Faced with so many choices, many people find comfort in harking back to their ancestral roots or in bringing a favorite vacation spot home. Home and, the very heart of it, the kitchen are often designed to embody the aesthetics of the Old World. Today's designs may invoke the casual elegance of the Italian countryside, the classic formality of Roman design, the sophisticated splendor of Parisian parlors, or the culinary culture of Provence. Some yearn for the stately order of formal British drawing rooms or the casual, garden culture of English country estates. Then there are the fans of Spanish and Moorish influence, those who like the Delft tiled effects of Dutch design, or the clean and earthy lines of Scandinavian sensibilities.

The designs in this book are in no way predicated upon historic, Old World kitchens. After all, we no longer cook over open fires. Rather than being places where servants worked slavishly, kitchens are now the magnetic center of the home, where friends and family members draw together. The kitchens in this book evoke a sense of the past, of its materials and textures, colors and themes, while providing state-of-the-art cooking and dining spaces that fit into today's lifestyles.

In a society that values uniqueness, each design expresses the personality and vision of its designer. The images shown are simply launching points for the creation of entirely new kitchens that draw upon old traditions to express something completely new.

Courtesy of StarMark Cabinetry

True to Tuscany

A yearning for Tuscan design reflects an age-old desire shared by Italians, who like us, yearned to escape politics, intrigue, and the crush of humanity for a more simple country retreat. For generations, the rustic second homes of Tuscany were furnished simply and casually. Many of these historic country houses are available for rent today, and an escape to the "Tuscan Sun" embodies a dream that annually draws thousands to this Mediterranean province of Italy.

The goal is to reconnect with the earth and immerse oneself in the tones, smells, tastes, and textures of hillside Tuscan towns. The ideal includes a generations-old home, its crumbling stone walls in tune with a lush garden, its sturdy marble floors, wood furnishings, and wrought-iron accessories an enduring element among sun-washed hillsides.

Courtesy of Waverly, F. Schumacher & Co.

The outside comes in for a Tuscan feel, with windows left open to allow natural light to illuminate the room. When possible, high ceilings with exposed beams create an open airy feeling.

Faux painting techniques can be used to create a sense of age and depth, while wooden surfaces tend to have natural finishes or to be antiqued. Open shelving and free-standing cupboards are naturals, and a long wooden table for family dining is the favorite accessory. Tumbled marble tiles and a great range hood are decorative accessories that complement a Tuscan setting, and colorful ceramics and shiny copper make apt adornments.

For authenticity, if you can squeeze a wood-fired oven into your kitchen, it will be complete, and the stage set for margarita pizzas, fresh breads and sides of garden-ripened tomatoes and basil with fresh cheeses and aged wines.

Ann C. Sherman Photography

A hand-painted hood thematically evokes a Mediterranean mood. *Courtesy of JAY Interiors*

The informality of open storage under an island worktable, and the casual display of artwork atop a range hood create a sense of the old family home. Carved mouldings, earth tones, and textured surfaces help to create a sunny, Tuscan mood. *Courtesy of Wood Mode, Inc.*

A contrast of dark and white plays against the golden background of wall in this room. The stucco hood, ornamented with a beautiful wood cutout, commands center stage. A marble sink lends this kitchen its heirloom appeal, set amidst cabinetry where the two-tone finish adds antique effect. *Courtesy of Downsview Kitchens*

11

A Tuscan Decorating theme evokes Old World styling. The hearth becomes a focal area, with pull-out storage on either side of the range, and many types of storage with easy access below.
Courtesy of StarMark Cabinetry

Warm stucco walls give this kitchen its inviting Mediterranean flair. A hand-hewn slab of stone tops a central island, and an elegant hood caps a range, backed by low-maintenance decorative tile. *Courtesy of Facings of America*

A pizza oven in a stucco wall place this kitchen firmly atop Italian roots. A garden entry invites one to take the meal outside where a warm Mediterranean climate awaits. *Courtesy of Mid Continent Cabinetry*

13

A brick floor starts this room off on the right rustic note for a historic kitchen. Antique table, chairs, and butcher block in the center of the room are in keeping with the theme, while the cook is backed up with state-of-the-art cooking facilities for a wonderful marriage of old and new. *Courtesy of Viking Range Corporation*

Red accents add flame to a warm, wood-tone setting. An underline of slate tile flooring is repeated in the backsplash. *Courtesy of Merillat*

An arched window might easily encompass a view of Italy's hill towns, while inside a great hood crowns the cook's hearth. Warm stone and wood fill this room with earth tones. A massive central island capped with granite makes this mammoth kitchen the centerpiece of the home. *Courtesy of Crystal Cabinet Works*

An idyllic gourmand's retreat is set within this cavernous stone space, where cooking and dining space were artfully coupled with wine storage. Leaded windows, great beamed ceilings, hand-blown lamp globes, and furniture-quality cabinetry display the exquisite attention to detail lavished on this room. *Courtesy of Wood Mode, Inc.*

Warm, earthen tones were carefully selected and blended throughout this kitchen to create a harmonious atmosphere. European flair is introduced through the hood styling and the round-top windows that flank this fixture, along with the diamond motif backsplash.
Courtesy of KraftMaid Cabinetry

Warm food themes add accent to this classic, paneled kitchen.
Carved details in the fine cabinetry further embellish the setting.
Courtesy of Merillat

An Italian sensibility is evident in the shape of the range hood, the metalwork on the chairs, and the artful glass light fixtures.
Courtesy of Janet Green Interior Design

Granite countertop is continued in the backsplash as well as a skirt treatment for the sink area. Two tones of cabinetry break up the outline of the kitchen. *Courtesy of Canyon Creek Cabinetry*

A kitchen becomes the wall in a larger living area, inviting friends and family closer with a long stretch of counter. *Courtesy of Canyon Creek Cabinetry*

homeowner in Atlanta wanted her new kitchen to evoke a sense of her ancestral Italy. A wood-burning hearth, imported tile, and heirloom-quality cabinetry now combine to transport her daily. *Courtesy of Jackie Naylor Interiors*

Photography by Phil Bekker

Photography by Phil Bekker

Stone walls and floor evoke the coastal regions of Southern France. A cook's dream, the range and oven, spice racks, and ample working space were set aside in a lighted alcove. Stand-alone cabinetry furnishings evoke an ancestral heritage, and emphasize the working nature of this kitchen space. *Courtesy of Mid Continent Cabinetry*

A dark finish on the cabinetry improves the aged look as well as bringing out detailing. The cabinetry enhances the feeling of individual pieces of furniture through multiple heights and depths, as well as a hearth hood over the range. Heavy columns on the corners of the island further the furniture feel. A creative tile backsplash was installed over the sink area. *Courtesy of Fieldstone Cabinetry*

A kitchen set up to create two basic work areas – one for a cook preparing hot foods on the range, another that works more as food prep and casual serving areas. Both share a central sink. *Courtesy of Canyon Creek Cabinetry*

A distressed finish on the cabinetry and a rag-like faux finish wallpaper work together to add antiquity to a country kitchen. *Courtesy of Waverly, F. Schumacher & Co.*

Classic Roman

In today's interior design world, neo-classical styles hark back to the great buildings of Greece and Rome. Building upon the Greek traditions that incorporated columns and triangular pediments, the Italians contributed arches and domes. These elements have been revived time and again throughout history, and their presence lends a sense of establishment, order, and classicism to architecture, whether inside or out.

The great public buildings of the United States tend to reflect the mathematical proportions established by Italian architect Andrea Palladio (1508-1580), and invariably exhibit columns, arches, domes, and triangles.

Dentil moulding is an adornment indicative of the style, as are carved medallions, urns, grapes, and grape leaves. Other accessories for a classically styled kitchen might include hand-blown glass like that produced in Murano, Italy, or marble countertops and stonework, like that quarried in the country and shaped by fine Italian craftsmen for countless generations.

Look for carved columns facing cabinetry and classically turned columns supporting the ceiling. Arched openings such as doorways, window surrounds, and hood openings over ranges are also indicative. Most importantly, a classically styled kitchen is orderly and balanced in its arrangement, creating a sense of measure in its presentation.

The great grape is celebrated in framed art and pretty carved details in the cabinetry and pulls, while olives adorn the dinnerware. This kitchen is a homage to all that is great about a classic Italian meal. *Courtesy of Crystal Cabinet Works*

Italian travertine defines the floor, its diagonally construed parquet pattern adding an illusion of extra space to this kitchen. A rooster atop the granite island/eating bar becomes a central character in the room. *Courtesy of Facings of America*

A heritage of great architecture is reflected in fluted columns, crown moulding, and raised panel mounding on the cabinetry. A spaghetti faucet pulls out behind the range for perfect pasta making, and an open cabinet below reveals an arsenal of cookware for the passionate chef. *Courtesy of Crystal Cabinet Works*

A faux doorway opens the way to the garden path, beautifully framed in moulding to match the custom cabinetry in this enormous kitchen. Richly carved corbels support the archway over the imaginary opening, as well as the practical hood enclosure of the range and the marble counter capping a great central work island. *Courtesy of Downsview Kitchens*

Right:
The influence of the ancient Romans is felt in this kitchen, with a marbled column and dentil moulding crowning the room. Colorful pottery and tile adds zest to the space, and a wealth of canister lighting and suspended lights over the central cook station create a bright workspace. *Courtesy of Crystal Cabinet Works*

French Provincial

Who has traveled through Provence, France's southernmost province, and failed to come home filled with thoughts of redecorating. The reasons are obvious including the distinctive primary colors and pleasing patterns of their textiles and porcelains. And then there's the overwhelming culinary culture that permeates the region, from fine wines, cheeses, and breads to a garden culture of fresh produce and long-lingering meals. Provence offers us a vision of a more relaxed world, where meals are great social events, presented with little fanfare, and carried out over the course of hours. Food is digested with healthy measures of laughter, in comfortable chairs and unpretentious surroundings. The memories of these moments are softened, like a Monet painting, with rust red and cobalt blue against a soft background of hay fields, lazy seaside tones, and great swathes of blooming lavender, punctuated with sunny yellow. Casual, rustic furnishings fit in amidst painted plaster walls, delicate carved wood details, and beamed ceilings overlooking natural stone floors. Most importantly, elements of basic cookery are proudly displayed – copper pots, herbs and garlic, and a great hearth or, in the modern vernacular, a hooded range that harks back to the great stone fireplace.

A handsome kitchen like this would be at home anywhere. The ample hearth area over the range is evocative of olden days, as is the hanging pot and basket holder over the island. The influence of country craftsmanship is felt in the ball feet on the block legs created to help support the island. Riveted copper plating protects those legs, as well as the corners of the expansive wood counter atop the central workstation. *Courtesy of Crystal Cabinet Works*

Colorful tiles establish a sense of Southern France in this open, country kitchen plan. With serving ware at the ready, this room is ready to comfortably seat and feed eight for family-style meals prepared with loving care. A wonderful mix of lighting adds glow to the room, from a picture window for generous daylight, to shaded sconces by the range and a filigreed chandelier. *Courtesy of Bis Bis Imports, Boston*

Blue walls and country antique furnishings set the tone for this spacious, casual kitchen. A central worktable is utilitarian for food preparation and as a family gathering spot for informal meals. *Courtesy of Wood Mode, Inc.*

Rich details like stenciling, mixed tiles, and appropriate textiles give this room a "been-here-forever" feeling. How else could so much thought have been fitted into this room, from the coffered ceiling with heavy timber beams to the hand-painted hood? Pretty seat cushions come straight from Provence, and hence you are transported when seated here. *Courtesy of Susan Cohen Associates, Inc.*

A sense of old meets new characterizes this kitchen, with modern appliances and glass-front display side-by side with antiqued white cabinetry and artful whicker furnishings. *Courtesy of KraftMaid Cabinetry*

The owners have adorned their glass-front grain bins with painted pottery, adding a hint of Provence to this spacious kitchen setting. *Courtesy of KraftMaid Cabinetry*

Pretty blue tiles, a collection of culinary antiques, and the welcoming informality of this room place it smack dab in the center of France's rural paradise. This cook's kitchen includes an expansive range and cleverly concealed modern appliances. In the nook under the stairs, wine storage, microwave, and refrigerator each find a place, as do cookbooks and, cleverly concealed wastebasket behind the angled pull drawer at the far left. The Provincial-region's pretty Quimper pottery is proudly displayed throughout the room, and tiles of the region act as backsplash. *Courtesy of Plain & Fancy Custom Cabinetry*

While blue and white pottery stands out on display, it's the pretty dinnerware displayed in the cabinet that gives this kitchen its sense of Provincial place. *Courtesy of Crystal Cabinet Works*

Plate racks over the sink once served to drip-dry the dishes. Today they are primarily for display. A wonderful focal point is created in the recessed range top area, with a lighted wood surround complete with carved corbels. *Courtesy of Wellborn Cabinet, Inc.*

Punched tin door inserts create focal points in this bright, open kitchen. *Courtesy of StarMark Cabinetry*

Don Santos Photography

A soft blue background allows the pastel and earthen tones of pottery pieces to take center stage in this wonderful kitchen. Pretty elements like colored glass crystals suspended from the chandelier, hand-painted porcelain canisters, and a goose on the countertop, add flair and femininity to the environment. *Courtesy of L'Interieur by J. Crawford / cabinetry by D'Laughlin Kitchens*

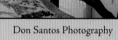
Don Santos Photography

Ceramic and wood add depth and texture to this pretty kitchen. *Courtesy of KraftMaid Cabinetry*

The classic colors of Provence – red, yellow, and blue – play throughout this wonderful, L-shaped kitchen area, with a half-wall that serves as an eating counter. *Courtesy of Village, F. Schumacher & Co.*

Ornamental carving in the maple cabinetry helps set the stage, wherein the fruits of the vineyard are celebrated. *Courtesy of The Hardwood Council*

A favorite add-on to any kitchen is the butler's pantry. This one's worthy of sharing with company, as the colors and décor transport one to the beautiful French countryside. *Courtesy of Interior Decisions, MC*

Marisa Pellegrini Photography

Designer Dee Morrissey used two cabinet finishes and a light green granite countertop to set a soft and friendly tone for a kitchen formal in design, but child friendly for a family. A planked farmhouse table adds to the informality, and short stools invite family and friends to the island counter. All of the appliances were carefully encased in cabinet finishes, and a stone floor was selected for its durability. *Courtesy of Morrissey & Thompson-Ryan Interior Design*

Marisa Pellegrini Photography

Cabinetry provides the effect of fine paneling around a stone range surround. A sink area, likewise, gets a beautiful frame from richly detailed wood wall and floor units and exquisite crown moulding. *Courtesy of Downsview Kitchens*

An altar to the almighty grape, this kitchen plants its roots firmly in country soil with massive turned legs on the island, and an earthen-toned tile floor. Carved corbels and moulding evoke a rich heritage, complemented by a distressed antique finish and tumbled tile backsplash.
Courtesy of Plain & Fancy Custom Cabinetry

Warm wood tones surround a central island and cook center finished with sage tones and carved details. Hanging cookware, dried flowers, and herbs add to the informality of the beautiful setting. *Courtesy of Kountry Kraft, Inc.*

A warm flagstone floor underlines a room rich in detail. At its center is a mantel-like hood, hand-carved to portray grapevines. *Courtesy of Crystal Cabinet Works*

Picture windows play the predominant role in a kitchen where the view is everything. To compete with the splendor outside, a beautiful backsplash and wrought-iron chandeliers were chosen for their head-turning quality. *Courtesy of Canyon Creek Cabinetry*

Parisian Splendor

The extravagance of silk, gilt, and glitter help define the ideal established by Louis XIV in his grand palace of Versailles. Today, a Paris apartment still represents the highlife, fit for movie stars and monarchs alike.

In the kitchen, this ideal has been translated into heavily carved furniture and cabinetry, shimmering chandeliers, and shameless helpings of scarlet, gold, emerald, and mirror-finish black.

A sophisticated, Parisian environment draws on many influences, from baroque and rococo to neoclassical and art deco, as well as the antiqued effects of Mediterranean and Old World styles. Timeworn elegance is every bit as important as the bright reflections and the comfort of velvets and luxurious brocades that beg to be incorporated into the decor. Toile and Oriental carpets are among the acceptable textiles for a sophisticate, and themes from *fleurs de lis* to roosters might be tapped, as well as impressionist paintings or pastoral scenes from the Bordeaux region.

Adopting Parisian sensibilities indicates an owner's desire to be bit more formal, while inviting the gay influence of the cabaret.

Carved corbels on the island and hearth, as well as crown moulding, posts, and onlays draw on historic woodworking traditions. The addition of textured glass in the mullion insert doors makes a rich statement, as well. *Courtesy of Fieldstone Cabinetry*

A variety of French periods adds a European touch to this multi-functioning family kitchen. *Courtesy of Sabrina Balsky Interior Design*

An antiqued finish on the cabinetry adds the patina of age to this handsome kitchen space. The eleven-foot ceilings accentuate the custom hand finishing of the cabinets. *Courtesy of Sabrina Balsky Interior Design*

Egg ornaments and a lovely wallpaper create primary adornments for this galley kitchen. Louvered windows create ventilation on the outside wall, their shape and luminosity mirrored in glass-fronted cabinets on the pantry wall opposite. A tiny bump-out creates a working ledge above the microwave, while leaving room for the convenient island complete with seating. *Courtesy of Crystal Cabinet Works*

Sophisticated detailing gives this kitchen its formal flair, from
floral wood carvings surrounding the range, to stately carved
columns supporting the expansive central island's granite surface.
Courtesy of KraftMaid Cabinetry

Jim Montgomery Photography ©2006

Inspired by a trip to Paris, designer Blue Harris brought home the ideal to her tiny kitchen. An enormous map of Paris on the ceiling commemorates this great city, circa Marie Antoinette, while walls of French Mustard add cheer to this charming space. Black and white antique plates serve as décor throughout. A pair of antique etched mirrors crowns the sink. *Courtesy of Blue Designs, Interiors & Antiques*

Ira Montgomery Photography, ©2006

Top: A distressed finish and antique toile print treatments create a fascinating kitchen sink surround, backed by brick. A central island includes lion corbels and hand-painted details.

Bottom: An oil painting is a perfect hood ornament in a room that seems composed of treasured heirlooms. *Courtesy of a karen black company*

Dripping in detail – applied wood ornament, a crystal chandelier, and granite countertops – this kitchen typifies the sophistication found in today's kitchen design. *Courtesy of JAY Interiors*

Ann C. Sherman Photography

A soft color palette of creams with subtle green and russet accents plays throughout this elegant kitchen, where an abundance of detail waits to be discovered. *Courtesy of Pauline Vastardis Interiors*

English Formal

Cabinet styles today have transformed kitchen storage into fine woodwork. Today's kitchens often resemble the beautifully paneled drawing rooms enjoyed by highborn gentlemen a century ago. Rich finishes and styles create a sense of 19th century finery in today's more formal kitchens.

The result is a place where one would be proud to entertain the boss. After all, today's gatherings tend to center in the kitchen, whereas the gatherings of yesteryear were conducted in formal parlors and dining rooms, while servants brought food from a kitchen no one ever saw. For those who entertain for business, a beautiful kitchen is practically a requirement, even if a caterer has been engaged. Moreover, the scale and equipment found in many kitchens today allow the caterer to work on site, and the quality of the food is greatly improved by its freshness.

Formal elegance was created with a rich finish on the cabinetry and a coffered ceiling. *Courtesy of Merillat*

Detailed woodwork in the cabinetry and a beautifully etched slate backsplash recall the honed craftsmanship of the Northern European regions. Carved rope insets adorn the crown moulding and fancy fretwork and turned legs are among the many fine details. *Courtesy of Plain & Fancy Custom Cabinetry*

Marble and turned legs frame an island that looks like an antique chest of drawers. Open shelving and fine woodwork are reminiscent of olden times. *Courtesy of Canyon Creek Cabinetry*

Formal cabinetry alludes to the gentrified life in this spacious kitchen. *Courtesy of KraftMaid Cabinetry*

A soft, creamy yellow cabinetry was given a warm brown glaze to soften its glow. The cabinet heights and depths were staggered to add interest to the paneled room effect that creates a generous allowance of storage space. Classic mouldings and turned posts add to the refined atmosphere of the cabinet installations. A black, glass-top range was skillfully blended with dark countertop, and almost disappears. The elliptical arch above seems more ornamental than the useful ventilation hood it disguises. *Courtesy of Wood Mode, Inc.*

A wealth of wall cabinetry provides storage, and allows the dedication of one wall to the massive open range and hood. *Courtesy of Downsview Kitchens*

A cathedral ceiling with exposed beams and celestory windows evokes a sense of centuries ago. The kitchen has been furnished elegantly in cabinetry fashioned in the tradition of fine furniture, with carved valances, footed stands, and olive burl parquet insert panels. Open shelving and wall cabinets with mullion glass doors add to the airy atmosphere. *Courtesy of Wood Mode, Inc.*

Photos by Dave Adams

A tiny kitchen packs a lot of punch, with rich custom cabinetry complete with a built-in wine cellar, glass-fronted display cabinets, and state-of-the-art appliances. *Courtesy of Delicate Design*

Antiqued white cabinetry provides a framework for the interplay of rose and grey elements. There is a beautiful balance of color, from the stone floor tiles to the marble-inlay counters, tile backsplash behind the stove, and the ceiling. *Courtesy of Downsview Kitchens*

Lighting is an important accent in a room, providing both a style statement and proper task illumination for each work area. *Courtesy of Kitchen Concepts & Roomscapes, Inc.*

Clean lines create a sense of British decorum in this thoughtfully laid out kitchen. The beloved garden comes indoors, perched on three shelves set aside for flowers. Paneling conceals a stainless steel refrigerator, and pull-out shelves increase the storage space. A buffet wraps an opposite corner, creating storage and display. The arched panel over the oven and range evokes the hearth in a paneled room. *Courtesy of Plain & Fancy Custom Cabinetry*

Art tiles and prized pottery pieces provide ornament in this handsome kitchen. A central island provides contrast to the creme wall cabinets. *Courtesy of Canyon Creek Cabinetry*

Footed base cabinets create the illusion of free-standing furniture in this kitchen, where work and storage space have been maximized with custom cabinetry. *Courtesy of Canyon Creek Cabinetry*

From the molding encrusted, cream-colored cabinetry to the keystone atop the "hearth" surround, this kitchen is packed with exquisite detailing. *Courtesy of Downsview Kitchens*

Beautiful tapered columns stained to match the woodwork create a wonderful entry and a sense of space for a kitchen set jewel-like within an open floorplan. Broad stretches of white granite countertop offer inviting gathering spots as well as workspace. *Courtesy of Divine Kitchens LLC*

A chamfered ceiling and like-molded cabinetry create a formal framework for this gathering space. The central island offers a wonderful wooden workspace for the chef, and an immaculate, raised area where friends and family can sample or help. Among the many amenities is a retractable cookbook holder and a beautiful custom designed pie safe. *Courtesy of Kitchens by Design*

Tudor Elements

The nostalgia for the country in England can take the form of the old half-timbered houses that dotted both city and country for centuries. Prior to the 17th century, when England was a grand oak forest, the predominate method of house building involved hand-hewing great timbers from oak, using them to build supportive frames, then filling in the missing spaces with some form of plaster. The result was a black-and-white timber-frame architecture, the frame revealed in a dark stain, often with extra timbers added for decorative effect. Inside, great oaken beams were revealed supporting the ceiling or roof, and sometimes forming the walls and support columns.

This timber-frame look is enormously popular in upscale homes today, and no more so than in the kitchen, where exposed beams add warmth and provide perfect props for hanging herbs and culinary tools.

To complement this, brick and plaster are often incorporated, as well as rustic, sturdy furnishings. Mullioned windows, preferably with the small diamond panes popularized during the Tudor Revival periods, can be used in glass-fronted cabinetry as well as to frame exterior views. An open hearth completes the look, often imitated in the form of a towering range hood capping an ultra-modern, professional-quality appliance.

A stone surround supports a handsome wood hood in this elegant eat-in kitchen. A rich wood finish is capped by black countertops, and the shining black central range. *Courtesy of Mid Continent Cabinetry*

Ceiling beams recall the historic architecture of England, and the furnishings evoke the taste of lords and ladies. *Courtesy of Kraft-Maid Cabinetry*

Mullioned windows recall the Tudor mansions that dot the English countryside, and rich colors indoors create a sense of establishment, updated with modern, stainless steel appliances. *Courtesy of Viking Range Corporation*

Two angles reveal how stylish openings and storage were doled out in equal measure for a kitchen that gracefully wraps a huge central island. *Courtesy of Canyon Creek Cabinetry*

Tudor styling is expressed in wood beams stained dark and paired with formal cabinetry. Open shelving with arched valances highlights the symmetrical design of the wall cabinets that flank the range hood. Wicker baskets in a base cabinet add a practical yet Old World look, while wall cabinets with leaded glass inserts maintain the room's overall sense of elegance. An archway sheathed in a stone finish creates a sense of history in the portal between kitchen and dining areas, repeated above the window. *Courtesy of Wood Mode, Inc.*

Dual center islands characterize this dream kitchen. An expansive cook center inset beneath an arch and accented with decorative tile is one of many astounding focal points within the room. The eye is drawn up to wood beams within a coffered ceiling, and circular highlight windows that augment a flood of natural light from an adjacent glass wall. A bank of tall cabinets conceals a refrigerator and pantry that update the room, while a massive iron chandelier grounds it firmly in the aesthetics of the Old World. *Courtesy of Wood Mode, Inc.*

A wonderfully rich kitchen boasts no end of fine craftsmanship, starting with the floor itself, a large-scale parquet fashioned from the mixed mediums of stone and wood. Beautifully mullioned glass-front display cabinets circle round this spacious kitchen, and a mixed finish on the cherry cabinetry enhances the antique effect of the furnishings. *Courtesy of Wood Mode, Inc.*

English Country

In the popular take on English Country today, the garden comes in to mingle with simply styled antique furnishings in a casual, cottage-like atmosphere. British cottages were historically the domain of the agricultural workers and simple folk. Besides foliage and floral art, an English Country feel is accomplished with handmade, folk arts, worn fabrics, and splashes of color. Old and new are mixed in for the cottage look, with family heirlooms holding a proud place in the décor. Distressed cabinetry and pine plank tables are perfect furnishings. The sought-after effect is an overall feeling of cozy, soft and quaint. That atmosphere accounts for the broad appeal this style holds in the marketplace today.

An antique dresser fitted with a new wood counter top forms a wonderful accent piece for this kitchen outfitted like an English garden room. *Courtesy of Village, F. Schumacher & Co.*

Informal, knotty woods were chosen for the cabinetry and coffered ceiling, adding country casual to a classic setting. Modern in its application, a gas hearth harks back to the fireside of yesteryear. *Courtesy of Canyon Creek Cabinetry*

This kitchen could be dressed up or down. The owners chose to soften semi-formal cabinetry with informal basketry and antiques, along with the inviting presence of a kitchen table. *Courtesy of KraftMaid Cabinetry*

The harlequin pattern on the floor boards is repeated in a whimsical window treatment. Country touches and mixed cabinetry finish complete the casual atmosphere for this comfortable kitchen. *Courtesy of KraftMaid Cabinetry*

An apple-red theme creates an informal accent repeated throughout this warm, vanilla kitchen. Bonsai-scale pine and a framed collection of spoons reflect two British passions: the garden, and exotic travels. *Courtesy of Civility Design*

Crown moulding unites multiple depths and heights of cabinet elements. Beaded paneling, shelf corbels, and bun feet add texture and weight to the Old World feel. *Courtesy of StarMark Cabinetry*

Wood corbels, glass doors, and generous use of copper gives the feeling that this kitchen has been a gathering place for generations. *Courtesy of StarMark Cabinetry*

Glass tile, a chandelier sparkling with real flame, and other craftsman touches such as mullioned glass display cases add character and warmth to this Arts and Crafts era kitchen. *Courtesy of Merillat*

Spanish Style

For those seeking something a little more exotic and spicy, Spanish style has broad appeal, especially in areas of the Southwest, where the bold colors of the Mediterranean are right at home in the New World.

Real stucco or rag-rolled walls with tones of gold and red are often employed to create a warm environment, underlined by terra cotta or other earth-toned tiles. Accessories include hand-wrought iron chandeliers and displays of distinctive porcelain wares.

A Moorish influence characterized by arched openings is right at home and adds the right touch of architecture to a room.

Select cross-cut travertine flooring amidst stucco-finished walls creates a Mediterranean atmosphere for this warm, inviting kitchen. *Courtesy of Facings of America*

A massive central cutting table creates a focal point in this setting. An arched opening to the room beyond, and a wrought-iron chandelier add a touch of Spain to the atmosphere. *Courtesy of Canyon Creek Cabinetry*

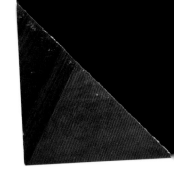

Moorish arches and a tapered range hood add Spanish flair to this kitchen. A central island presents a half-round table extension for casual dining. *Courtesy of Canyon Creek Cabinetry*

Stucco walls and tiled floor recall warm Mediterranean climates, while the arched doorways and windows remember a Moorish influence. Antique furnishings blend beautifully with modern appliances finished in a cobalt blue befitting a seaside abode. *Courtesy of Viking Range Corporation*

Further Abroad

The images in this section explore other European influences on contemporary kitchen designs, from Delft-ware tiles to the soft, natural environments of the Scandinavian countries. The goal, of course, is to pick and choose looks and elements that bring you that sense of timeless appeal.

An antique French lighting fixture creates European flair, while large sandstone pavers bring old world materials into this kitchen space. The counters and backsplash are blue granite from Brazil. The island is solid walnut, crafted on site. *Courtesy of Sabrina Balsky Interior Design*

European styling in the cabinetry, textiles, and lighting add continental flair to a log cabin setting. *Courtesy of Town & Country Cedar Homes*

Tiled backdrop, granite, and cabinetry in variations of white heighten the perception of space within this small kitchen. These age-old materials, paired with contemporary steel appliances, give Mediterranean design a contemporary twist. *Courtesy of Divine Kitchens LLC*

Tile frames for wood and glass base cabinetry give this room its distinctive character. The sense is of stepping into a kitchen long in service, though updated with modern features. *Courtesy of Bis Bis Imports, Boston*

Practically tiled in blue and white, a kitchen's open shelves stand at the ready, offering up serving options. *Courtesy of Bis Bis Imports, Boston*

Pretty blue tiles span a tall wall in this kitchen, while an old-fashioned treatment creates an ice-box effect for the refrigerator under an arched nook. A glass chandelier adds old-fashioned elegance to the space, designed for both cooking efficiency and a spacious place where the family can gather. *Courtesy of Bis Bis Imports, Boston*

A beautiful blend of cultures combine in this room, from a wrought-iron chandelier and backsplash tiles with Spanish flair, to marble countertops typical of Italian craftsmanship, to woodwork befitting British craftsmen. *Courtesy of Canyon Creek Cabinetry*

A sense of Scandinavia is evoked in this Swedish Country kitchen, characterized by a rich, black-glaze finish on cherry. The diagonal lattice detail in the doors on either side of the cook center are unique, as is the cutout work in the valance topping the plate rack over the sink. *Courtesy of Wood Mode, Inc.*

A sunny kitchen is set within the airy surrounds of a timber-framed room. The tiled fresco behind the range and the weathered pitchfork above evoke the farm fields of a gentle region, and the beloved blue and yellow dinnerware of the region is proudly displayed.
Courtesy of Plain & Fancy Custom Cabinetry

Resource Guide

Following is contact information for the designers and manufacturers who contributed images to this book. The author wishes to thank them all for sharing their talents and vision, and helping to define style for those searching for the look perfect for their home and lifestyles. Please contact them for advice and guidance in creating your own Old World kitchen.

Bis Bis Imports, Boston
4 Park Plaza
Boston, MA 02116
617-350-7565
www.bisbis.com

Blue Designs Interiors & Antiques
6152 Bandera
Dallas, TX 75225
214-373-1283
www.texas-designers.com

Canyon Creek Company
16726 Tye Street SE
Monroe, WA 98272
206-674-0800
www.canyoncreek.com

Charlotte Comer Interiors, Inc.
5609 Vickery Boulevard
Dallas, TX 75225
214-953-0855
www.charlottecomerinteriors.com

Civility Design
1515 N. Astor St.
Chicago, IL 60610
312-640-9529

Susan Cohen Associates, Inc.
2118 Wilshire Boulevard, Ste. 962
Santa Monica, CA 90403-5784
310-828-4445
www.susancohenassociates.com

Kitchen Concepts & Roomscapes, Inc.
159 Washington Street
Norwell, MA 02061
781-871-2400
www.roomscapesinc.com

Crystal Cabinet Works
1100 Crystal Drive
Princeton, MN 55371
800-347-5045
www.ccworks.com

Delicate Design
PO Box 293503
Sacramento, CA 95829
916-871-2892
www.Delicate-Design.com

Divine Kitchens LLC
40 Lyman Street
Westborough, MA 01581
508-366-5670
www.divinekitchens.com

Downsview Kitchens
2635 Rena Road
Mississauga, Ontario, Canada L4T 1G6
905-677-9354
www.downsviewkitchens.com

Facings of America
16421 North 90th Street
Scottsdale, AZ 85260

480-222-8480
www.facingsofamerica.com

Fieldstone Cabinetry
600 East 48th Street North
Sioux Falls, SD 57104
800-339-5369
www.fieldstonecabinetry.com

StarMark Cabinetry
600 East 48th Street North
Sioux Falls, SD 57104
800-594-9444
www.fieldstonecabinetry.com

Janet Green Interior Design
3003C Richmond Road
Texarkana, TX 75503
903-831-6617

The Hardwood Council
400 Penn Center Blvd., Suite 530
Pittsburgh, PA 15235
800.373.WOOD
www.hardwood.org

The Idea Company
865 Pond Meadow Road
Westbrook, CT 06498
860-399-5459

Jackie Naylor Interiors
4287 Glengary Dr. N.W.
Atlanta, GA 30342
404-814-1973

JAY Interiors
10614 Pagewood Lane
Dallas, TX 75230
214-691-0842

a karen black company
3013 N.W. 63rd
Oklahoma City, OK 73116
405-858-8333
www.akarenblackcompany.com

Kitchens by Design
65 Central Street
West Boylston, MA 01583
800-649-0309
www.kitchensbydesign.com

Kountry Kraft, Inc.
291 S Sheridan Road
PO Box 570
Newmanstown, PA 17073
610-401-0584
www.kountrykraft.com

KraftMaid Cabinetry
PO Box 1055
Middlefield, OH 44062
800-571-1990
www.kraftmaid.com

L'Interieur by J. Crawford
18A High Street
Westerly, RI 02891
401-348-0045
www.linterier-jcrawford.com

Mid Continent Cabinetry
3020 Denmark Ave., Suite 100
Eagan, MN 55121
651-234-3344
www.midcontinentcabinetry.com

Merillat
PO Box 1946
Adrian, MI 49221
www.merillat.com

Morrissey & Thompson-Ryan Interior
Design
29 Rt. 24 North Suite 215
Colts Neck, N.J. 07722
732-577-8884
www.mtrinteriors.com

Pauline Vastardis Interiors
300 Mill St. Suite 210
Moorestown, N.J. 08057
856-866-1625
www.pvinteriors.com

Plain & Fancy Custom Cabinetry
Route 501 and Oak Street
Schaefferstown, PA 17088
717-396-0200
www.plainfancycabinetry.com

Sabrina Balsky Interior Design
New York/Toronto/Florida
212-585-0441, 416-486-7879, 305-
935-0749

Village, FSC Wallcoverings
79 Madison Avenue
New York, NY 10016
212-213-7860
www.villagehome.com

Waverly, FSC Wallcoverings
79 Madison Avenue
New York, NY 10016
212-213-7860
www.decoratewaverly.com

Town & Country Cedar Homes
4772 U.S. 131 South
Petoskey, MI 49770
800-968-3178
www.cedarhomes.com

Interior Decisions, MC
140 Columbia Turnpike
Florham Park, NJ 07932
973-765-9013

Viking Range Corporation
111 Front Street
Greenwood, Mississippi 38930 USA
662-455-1200
www.vikingrange.com

Signature Kitchens & Baths of Charlotte
1926 Savannah Highway
Charleston, S.C. 29407
843-571-5720

Wellborn Cabinet, Inc.
38669 Highway 77
Ashland, AL 36251
256-354-7151
www.wellborn.com

Wood Mode, Inc.
One Second Street
Kreamer, PA 17833
877-635-7500
www.Wood-Mode.com